CONTENTS

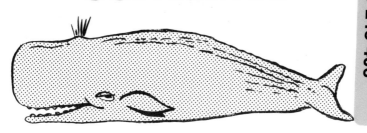

1. Animal Crackers   5

2. Beware of the Beast   11

3. Creature Comforts   17

4. Claws & Effect   23

5. Animal Rights . . . & Wrongs   29

6. Off the Beastly Beaten Path   36

7. Menagerie Madness   42

8. Down on the Funny Farm   49

9. Critter Litter   56

10. Buggy Belly Laughs   62

11. Zoo's Who?   67

12. Jest for the Halibut   73

13. Flying High   82

14. Tougher & Tougher   88

Index   94

1. ANIMAL CRACKERS

What two classes is the animal kingdom divided into?
The aardvarks and the aaren'tvarks.

MUFFY: What's a gnu?
DUFFY: Not much. What's a new with you?

What has antlers and eats cheese?
Mickey Moose.

What does a duck eat for snacks?
Cheese and quackers.

What do anteaters like on their pizza?
Ant-chovies.

What is the favorite drink of Australian bears?
Coca-Koala.

What do nuts chase after with little nets?
Peanut butter-flies.

What is a HIbVE?
A small bee in a big hive.

What did one caterpillar say to the other caterpillar?
Look before you creep.

What insect plays football?
A fumble bee.

What do bees chew?
Bumble gum.

Why do bees have sticky hair?
Because they always use honey combs.

What kind of weapon do bees use?
Bee-bee guns.

Where did Noah keep his bees?
In the ark-hives.

What animal hibernates on its head and meditates?
Yoga Bear.

What do you get if a little bear sits in a cornfield?
Corn on the cub.

What would you get if you crossed corn on the cob and a porcupine?
Something you could eat and pick your teeth with at the same time.

What would you get if you crossed a porcupine and an alarm clock?
A stickler for punctuality.

What would you get if you crossed a porcupine and a cactus?
Sore hands.

How do matadors write letters?
With bull point pens.

What would you get if you crossed a canary and a cat?
A peeping tom.

What is a cat's favorite pastime?
Listening to mewsic.

Why are birds so unhappy in the morning?
Because their bills are over dew.

What do you give a sick bird?
Tweetment.

What do insects take when they're ill?
Ant-ibiotics.

Why was the centipede uncomfortable?
He had athlete's foot.

What kind of apes talk a lot?
Blab-boons.

What language do elephants talk?
Mumbo jumbo.

What does the buffalo on a nickel stand for?
Because there's no room for it to sit down.

What is black and white and red all over?
An embarrassed Dalmation.

What do you get if you cross a frog and a dog?
A croaker spaniel.

When does a barking dog never bite?
While it's barking.

Why did the amoeba cross the road?
To get to the other slide.

Why was the amoeba prison so small?
Because it had only one cell.

What did the amoeba surf on?
A microwave.

What has webbed feet and fangs?
Count Quackula.

How do we know Dracula never got married?
Because he was a bat-chelor.

Why do vampires brush their teeth regularly?
To avoid bat breath.

Where do vampires find their victims?
In any neck of the woods.

What would you get if you crossed bats and a lonely-hearts club?

Lots of blind dates.

What would you get if you crossed a chicken and a ghost?

A poultrygeist.

Why couldn't the chicken find her eggs?

Because she mislaid them.

What does an evil chicken lay?

Devilled eggs.

Why did the chicken sit on the ax?

So she could hatchet.

How can you tell a dogwood tree?

By its bark.

What dog joins the Boy Scouts?

A beagle scout.

When does a horse neigh?

Whinny (when he) wants to.

What did one sheep say to the other sheep?

"After ewe."

What did the other sheep reply?

"Thank ewe."

2. BEWARE OF THE BEAST

What's invisible and smells like carrots?
Bunny breath.

How many skunks does it take to screw in a light bulb?
Quite a phew!

Why can't skunks keep secrets?
Because someone always gets wind of them.

What would you get if you crossed a crocodile and a camera?
A snapshot.

What would you get if you crossed a crocodile with one of the seven dwarfs?
An alligator with a short temper.

What would you get if you crossed a crocodile and an abalone?

A crocabolone.

What's the difference between a knight and Santa Claus's reindeer?

One slays the dragon, and the other's draggin' the sleigh.

What did one dragon say to the other dragon after fighting Sir Lancelot?

"Mother said there would be knights like this."

What do dragons do on Friday nights?

They let off steam.

What are young termites called?

Babes in the wood.

Why did the termite like groups of hotel rooms?
He had a suite tooth.

What did the boy feed his pet termite?
Table scraps.

What did the termite comedian say?
"This one will bring down the house."

What would you get if you crossed a trampoline and an iguana?
Leaping lizards.

What would you get if you crossed chit-chat and a rattler?
A prattlesnake.

What would you get if you crossed a chocolate bar and a snake that sheds?
Candy that molts in your mouth.

Why did the snake work for the government?
He wanted to be a civil serpent.

What is a snake's favorite opera?
"Wriggletto."

What kind of singers do they have in the forest?
Bearitones.

What do you call a grizzly half-buried in a snow bank?
A bear mid-drift.

What would you get if you crossed a bear and a skunk?
Winnie the Phew.

What would you get if you crossed a bear and a dog?
Winnie the Poodle.

What would you get if you crossed a cocker spaniel, a poodle and a ghost?
A cocker-poodle-boo.

Why did some dinosaurs live on land and others in water?
It was slink or swim.

What lives in the ocean and makes you an offer you can't refuse?
The Codfather.

What happened to the guy who used to be a werewolf?
He's all right now-oooooooooo.

What did the doctor reply when the man said he felt like a werewolf?
"Have a seat and comb your face."

What did the minister say when he saw bugs eating his cotton?
"I will fear no weevil."

What did the bee gunslinger say?
"Hive got you covered."

How do bloodhounds track down people?
By trail and error.

What kind of dogs work at the United Nations?
  Diplo-mutts.

Why did the family want to get rid of their new Great Dane?
  Because the big dog had the house broken before he was.

Why did the dog have a flat nose?
  He liked chasing parked cars.

If dogs have fleas, what do lambs have?
  Fleece.

What do lambs look for while shopping?
  Baaa-gains.

Why doesn't anyone like to bury an elephant?
  Because it is a huge undertaking.

Why didn't the little bird hurt himself when he fell out of the tree?

He used a sparrow-chute.

Why did the silly guy quit playing water polo?

Because his horse drowned.

What do you call a boxing canary who wins all its bouts?

A featherweight champion.

What would you get if you crossed a blender and a young goat?

A mixed-up kid.

What would you get if you crossed a goat and a sheep?

An animal that eats tin cans and gives back steel wool.

What would you get if you crossed a goat and a pig?

A crashing boar (bore).

What did the boy name his three pet boars?

Boarwinkle, Boar-is Karloff, and Boar-ed Stiff.

What would you call a cannibal who devoured his mother's sister?

An aunt-eater.

What would you get if you crossed a groundhog and a situation comedy?

Thirteen more weeks of jokes.

3. CREATURE COMFORTS

Where do frogs go when they need eyeglasses?
To the hoptician.

What did the motorist say to the hitchhiking frog?
"Hop in."

What is it called when you see frogs in front of your eyes?
A hoptical illusion.

What did one frog say to another?
"Time is sure fun when you're having flies."

What did the sign in the pet store window say?
"Buy one and get one flea."

What's the difference between a dog with fleas and a bored guest?
One is going to itch, and the other is itching to go.

What did the leftover turkey say after it was wrapped up?
"Foiled again."

Why did the chicken cross the road?
For fowl purposes.

What happened to the chickens that ate some racing forms?
The next morning they were laying odds.

What does "impeccable" mean?
It's something chickens can't eat.

What game do baby chickens play?
Peck-a-boo.

What publication do chickens read?
"Peep-le Magazine."

What is a hen's favorite book?
"Great Eggspectations" by Charles Chickens.

What would you get if you crossed a chicken and an old timepiece?
A grandfather cluck.

Why did Dr. Jekyll's chicken cross the road?
To get to the other Hyde.

What would you get if you crossed Dracula and a fish?
Cape Cod.

What would you get if you crossed a locksmith, a bird and Frankenstein?
A lock-nest-monster.

What do vampires play cards for?
High stakes.

What's the difference between a hairy dog and a painter?
One sheds his coat, and the other coats his shed.

What's the difference between a donkey and a stamp?
One you lick with a stick, and the other you stick with a lick.

What's the difference between a buffalo and a bison?
You can't wash your hands in a buffalo.

What did the farmer receive after buying a herd of bison?
A buffalo bill.

Where do baby cows eat?
In calfeterias.

What game do cows enjoy playing?
Moosical chairs.

What is the story about the cow bell?
I don't know. It hasn't been tolled.

What is a sheep's favorite newspaper?
"The Wool Street Journal."

What do you call a book about famous sheep?
"Ewe's Who."

What lives in the ocean and goes "Baaa" at ships?
A ewe-boat.

What do Arabian soldiers use to hide from their enemies?

Camelflage.

What did the boy say when his teacher told him that it takes over 1,000 camels each year to make paintbrushes?

"Isn't it amazing what they can teach animals to do?"

What would you get if you crossed a camel and a cow?

Lumpy milk shakes.

What would you get if you crossed a cow and an octopus?

An animal that milks itself.

What would you get if you crossed a pig and an octopus?

A football that throws itself.

Where did Tarzan work out?
At the jungle gym.

What household appliance eats ants and tapes TV shows?
The VCRdvark.

Why did the little gnu chew the furniture?
Because he was gnawty.

FLIP: If you were a big game hunter and suddenly met an alligator, a lion, and a rhinoceros, which animal would you get fur from?
FLOP: I'd get as fur from all of them as I could.

What do you call a rhino that drinks alcohol?
A wine-oceros.

What happens when a rhino's armor gets wet?
It rhinoce-rusts.

What is a snake's favorite meal?
Hiss and chips.

Why did the snake laugh so hard?
Because it had hissterics.

What kind of snakes come with cars?
Windshield vipers.

What did the coach say to his losing team of snakes?
"You can't venom all."

4. CLAWS & EFFECT

What did the cat say when it entered the saloon with its foot in a sling?

"I'm looking for the man who shot my paw."

What did they call kittens in the Old West?

Posse cats.

What's the difference between a pretty glove and a silent baby cat?

One is a cute mitten, and the other is a mute kitten.

What is the difference between a cat and a comma?

A cat has its claws at the end of its paws, and a comma has its pause at the end of a clause.

What did the boy do when his cat got run over by a
steamroller?

He just stood there with a long puss.

What do you call a fat cat?

A flabby tabby.

What did the psychiatrist call his scared pet?

A Freudy cat.

Where can you find a mind-reading cat?

At the E.S.P.C.A.

What did the mother turkey say to her misbehaving
daughter?

*"If your father could see you now, he'd turn over in his
gravy."*

What would you get if you crossed a Chinese cat with an alley cat?

A Peking Tom.

Where do Arabian cats live?

Near the Purrsian Gulf.

What's the difference between a frightened boy and a leopard's tail?

One is rooted to the spot, and the other is spotted to the root.

HUNTER #1: I just spotted a leopard!
HUNTER #2: Really? I thought they came that way.

What do leopards say after finishing a meal?

"That hit the spot."

Why do leopards have spotted coats?

Because tigers bought all the striped ones.

What do you get if you cross a needle and a tiger?

Pin stripes.

What kind of felines like bowling?

Alley cats.

What would you get if you crossed a grocery store and a big cat?

Check-out lions.

What would you get if you crossed a lion and a monastery?

A roaring friar place.

When is it hard to telephone the king of the jungle?
When the lion is busy.

What did the lion trainer look for in his contract?
A protection claws.

Why would a lion rather eat a man with a book than a man with a typewriter?
Because he knew that readers digest and writers cramp.

Why did the hunter, when attacked by a bull and a lion, shoot the lion first?
He figured he could always shoot the bull.

What is a literary lion?
A preditor-(predator)-in-chief.

What would you get if you crossed men's jewelry and a bobcat?
Cuff lynx.

Why do animals have to breed in order for the species to survive?
If they didn't breed, they'd suffocate.

How do we know a cat likes bad weather?
Because when it rains it purrs.

What is a cat burglar?
A purr-snatcher.

Why was the boy afraid of cats?
  Because he had clawstrophobia.

What newspaper advice column does Morris the Cat write?
  "Dear Tabby (Dear Abby)."

What's the difference between a cat and a match?
  One's light on its feet, and the other lights on its head.

How is a cat drinking milk like a track star?
  They both enjoy taking a few laps.

What happened when the cardplayer's cat swallowed a dime?
  There was money in the kitty.

What did the private detective do to the Manx cat?
  He put a tail on it.

What did the cat say when its tail got caught in a lawnmower?

"It won't be long now."

What might you get if your cat climbed into the washing machine?

A sock in the puss.

What did the pet store owner say when asked if he had any cats going cheap?

"No. All our cats go 'meow'."

Have you ever seen the Catskill mountains?

"No, but I've seen what they do to mice."

Why was the woman unhappy when her husband bought her a mink?

She didn't like cleaning the cage.

Why did the woman want four mink coats?

She thought they grew on fir (fur) trees.

What is one problem with the rat race?

Even if you win, you're still a rat.

5. ANIMAL RIGHTS ...& WRONGS

What happened to Little Bo Peep's sheep?
They were stolen by a crook.

Why did the lamb call the police?
He had been fleeced.

Why don't lambs get along together?
They have mutton in common.

How did the boy feel when he put on a lamb's wool sweater?
Sheepish.

Why shouldn't you tell whales secrets?
Because they're blubber mouths.

Why did the man quit smoking cold turkey?
He couldn't keep the cold turkey lit.

What do you get if you cross a turkey and a kangaroo?
An animal you can stuff on the outside.

What do you get if you cross an ostrich and a turkey?
A bird that buries its head in the mashed potatoes.

Why did the dog keep barking after it was fed?
It wanted a second yelping.

What kind of dog likes having its hair washed every day?
A shampoodle.

Why shouldn't you wash your rabbit with goat's milk?
Because you're not supposed to use that greasy kid stuff on your hare.

Why wouldn't the rabbit let the dentist give him novocaine?
Because he was an ether bunny.

What's the difference between an affectionate rabbit and an old lady?

One loves a pat and carrots, and the other loves a cat and parrots.

What's the difference between a man with a missing slipper and a detective trailing a criminal?

One suspects his dog, and the other dogs his suspect.

Where do you buy metal leashes for dogs?

In a chain store.

What did the toy store sign say?

"Don't feed the animals—they're already stuffed."

What sign did the grizzlies put up in the jungle?

"Support your right to arm bears (bear arms)."

What did the exterminator's sign say?

"Closed on fly day."

What animal is a cannibal?

The cow—because it eats its fodder.

What do you call a cow with no legs?

It doesn't matter what you call her; she still won't come.

Where are old cows exhibited?

In mooseums.

What is it called when cattle work well together?

Cowoperation.

What do kangaroos like to read?

Pocketbooks.

What do you get if you cross a dog and a kangaroo?

A pooch with a pouch.

What do you get if you cross a cantaloupe, a dog and an infant?

A melon collie baby.

What do you get if you cross chili pepper, a shovel and a collie?

Hot diggety dog.

What room did the squirrel get at the hotel?

The nutcracker's suite.

What is the otters' Golden Rule?

"Do unto otters as you would have them do unto you."

What do otters ride in?

Otter mobiles.

What did the father porcupine say to his son just before spanking him?

"This is going to hurt me more than it's going to hurt you."

Was the vampire disappointed when he came to a country road?

Yes, he was looking for a major artery.

What do vampires do at blood banks?

They make withdrawals.

How sick was the vampire?

He was in a grave condition.

How can you tell that a female deer needs money?

When she doesn't have a buck.

What is the strongest animal?

A race horse—because it can take hundreds of people for a ride at the same time.

What happened when the horse swallowed a dollar bill?

It bucked.

What do you call a horse that is born on the first day of the fourth month?

An April foal.

What type of race did the filly enter?

A marethon.

Why did Noah take four gnus on the ark?

So he could have some good gnus and some bad gnus.

How did the cat commit suicide?

It shot itself in the head nine times.

Where do cats go when they die?

To purr-gatory.

What fish is a serial killer?

Jack the Kipper.

What would you get if you crossed a stockbroker and an alligator?

An investigator.

What do you get if you cross a fisherman and a minister?

Someone who wants to save soles (souls).

What did the car mechanic do in the sardine factory?

Every three months he changed the oil.

What happened to the lazy workers in the sardine factory?

They were canned.

Why wouldn't the sardines ride the subway during rush hour?

They didn't like being packed in like commuters.

Why do baby birds in a nest always agree?

Because they don't want to have a falling out.

Who fights for equal rights for chickens?

A chicken libber.

How did the donkey live?

On burro'd time.

6. OFF THE BEASTLY BEATEN PATH

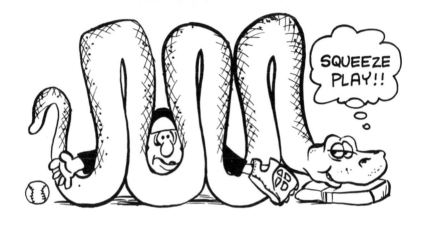

What sign was on the boa constrictor's cage at the zoo?
"Out to Crunch."

What happens when a snake acts silly?
It makes an asp of itself.

What would you call a beautiful snake that is a perfect "10"?
Boa Derek.

What would you get if you crossed a boa and some pasta?
Spaghetti that winds itself around a fork.

What do you get if you cross a boa and a sheep?
A wrap-around sweater.

Where do rabbits live during wartime?
In hare raid shelters.

What do rabbits think happens when you die?
They believe in a hare after.

What is a llama's favorite song?
"Llama Yankee Doodle Dandy."

Why did the silly hunter quit and go home?
He saw a sign that said "Bear Left."

What condominiums do Chinese bears live in?
Panda-monium.

Why should you never trust a bear with your date?
He might run off with your honey.

What monster made friends with the three bears?
Ghouldilocks.

What's the difference between Goldilocks and a genealogist?
A genealogist is interested in forebears.

What did the zookeeper's bumper sticker say?
"Old antelope breeders never die—they just begin a gnu."

How do we know deer and antelope are hard of hearing?
Because they never hear a discouraging word.

What did the sign at the deer crossing say?
"The buck stops here."

Who was the first deer astronaut?
Buck Rogers.

How did the doe win the animal race?
By passing the buck.

What did the mother deer say to the other deer?
"Time sure flies when you're having fawn."

How do deer call each other?
By tell-a-fawn.

What kinds of telephones do reptiles use?
Croco-dials.

What was the crow doing in the telephone booth?
Making a long distance caw.

Why do flamingos stand on one leg?
Because if they picked up the other leg, they'd fall over.

How can you tell if a motorcyclist is happy?
By the number of bugs on his teeth.

Why did the man sell his horseback-riding school?
Because business kept falling off.

What's the difference between a racehorse and a duck?
One goes quick on its legs, and the other goes quack on its eggs.

What did prehistoric carpenters use to cut through wood?
Dinosaws.

What did dinosaurs use to pay their bills?
Tyrannosaurus Checks.

What were dinosaurs like when they overworked?
Tyrannosaurus Wrecks.

What is slithery and good at counting?
An adder.

What was the atmosphere like in the snake pit?
There was adder (utter) confusion.

What did the octopus take with him on a camping trip?
Tent-acles.

What would you get if you crossed a policeman and an octopus?
A cop with eight long arms of the law.

What would you get if you crossed a clock and an octopus?
Either a clock with eight hands or an octopus that's really ticked off.

What would you get if you crossed a bale of hay and an octopus?

A broom with eight handles.

Why did the ape join the Marine Corps?

He wanted to learn about gorilla warfare.

What would you get if you crossed a gorilla, table tennis and a bell?

A King Kong Ping Pong Ding Dong.

What would you get if you crossed beaten egg whites and a sunburned monkey?

Meringue-tan.

What happened to the musician who used to be an organist?

His monkey died.

What animals are poor dancers?

Four-legged ones—because they have two left feet.

What is a vampire's favorite dance?

The fangdango.

What do you call a vampire's set of false teeth?

New-fang-led devices.

What's black and white and red all over?

A skunk with a diaper rash.

Why did the mother skunk take her baby to the doctor?

It was out of odor.

7. MENAGERIE MADNESS

... MISSING THE LAST BUS OF THE DAY, BUGS WAS *HOPPING MAD!!*

How do bunnies travel to work?
 By rabbit transit.

What is a rabbit's favorite car?
 A hutchback.

What's the difference between a unicorn and lettuce?
 One is a funny beast, and the other is a bunny feast.

What's the difference between a small animal who exercises too much and two pair of stockings?
 One is a sore fox, and the other is four socks.

What's the difference between a tailor and a horse trainer?
 One mends a tear, and the other tends a mare.

What is a horse's favorite sport?
Stable tennis.

What's the easiest way to make a slow horse fast?
Don't feed it.

What's in the middle of a popular horse magazine?
A monthly center foal.

How many animals did Moses take on the ark?
Moses didn't take any *on the ark. Noah did!*

What did Noah say while the animals were boarding the ark?
"Now I herd everything!"

How could Noah see the animals in the dark?
The ark had floodlights.

What did the boy flea say to the girl flea?
"Let's go out for a bite."

What's the difference between a girl and a mouse?
One charms he's, and the other harms cheese.

What is a mouse's favorite game?
Hide and squeak.

What did the mother mouse say when her baby fell onto the floor?
"Squeak to me."

"Doctor, Doctor, when I close my eyes I keep seeing Mickey Mouse!"
"Don't worry. You're just having Disney spells."

What happened when the boy porcupine met the girl porcupine?
They got stuck on each other.

Why can't peacocks be trusted?
Because they're always spreading tails (tales).

THE SKY IS FALLING...
THE SKY IS FALLING!!

AAAAKKK

What's gray on the inside and clear on the outside?
An elephant in a sandwich baggie.

What would you get if you crossed the Alps with elephants?
Mountains that never forget.

What would you get if you crossed a computer with an elephant?

A system with lots of memory.

What do you call a baby monkey?

A chimp off the old block.

What did the chimpanzee say when his sister had a baby?

"Well, I'll be a monkey's uncle!"

What is a gorilla's favorite musical?

"The Kong and I."

What did one monkey in the zoo say to the other monkey?

"You mean that I'm my keeper's brother?"

Where do monkeys get their information?
From the ape-vine.

What would you get if you crossed two ducks and three slices of bread?
A double-ducker sandwich.

What would you get if you crossed a duck and a garbage pit?
Down in the dumps.

What would you get if you crossed a garbage collector and an insect?
A litterbug.

What do you say to start a toy bear race?
Teddy, get set, go!

What would you get if you crossed a Bic and a short seabird?
A ballpoint pen-guin.

"Doctor, Doctor, I feel like a baby goat!"
"You've got to be kidding!"

How puzzled was the pig?
He was stymied.

What's the space adventure movie that was made about frogs?
"Star Warts."

Where do lambs like to go on vacation?
To the Baaahamas.

What would you call two lambs that have the same haircut?
Shear and shear alike.

Why did the chicken movie fan cross the road?
To see Gregory Peck.

What goes peck, peck, bang?
A chicken in a minefield.

What is the favorite newspaper of chickens?
"The National Henquirer."

What would you get if you crossed a chef and a rooster?
A cook-a-doodle-do.

What would you get if you crossed a pot and a rooster?
A crock-a-doodle-do.

What does a lazy rooster say?
"Cock-a-doodle-don't."

What kind of cheese is good on hot dogs?
Muttzarella.

What did the sign on the kennel say?
"Chock Full O' Mutts."

What happened when the cross-eyed dog chased a squirrel in the woods?
It barked up the wrong tree.

What kind of ice cream do dogs eat?
Pupsickles.

Why is an ink blotter like a lazy baby dog?
A blotter is an ink-lined plane, an inclined plane is a slope up, and a slow pup is a lazy dog.

8. DOWN ON THE FUNNY FARM

Where does baby corn come from?
The stalk brings it.

Where did the farmer keep his pet seahorse?
In the barn-acle.

How did the farmer find his missing cow?
He tractor down.

What did the farmer do when insects attacked his potato crop?
He kept his eyes peeled.

Why did the farmer cross his bees with fireflies?
He wanted them to work at night.

What do cattle athletes use to make them stronger?
Steeroids.

What's the difference between an angry crowd and a cow with a sore throat?
One boos madly and the other moos badly.

Where do milk shakes come from?
Nervous cows.

What do you get if you cross a cow with an Arab prince?
A milk sheik.

What do you get from pampered cows?
Spoiled milk.

What kind of milk did the forgetful cow give?
Milk of amnesia.

Is it easy to milk a cow?
Yes, any little jerk can do it.

What do you get from an Eskimo cow?
Cold cream.

What is a cattle rancher's favorite magazine?
"Breeder's Digest."

What other magazine do cattle like reading?
"Cowsmopolitan."

What did one cow say to the other cow?
"No moos is good moos."

Why did the farmer tell his son about the birds and the bees?
Because he didn't know anything about girls.

What is a sheep's favorite song?
"There Will Never Be Another Ewe."

What did the boy sheep say to the girl sheep?
"I only have eyes for ewe."

What did the sheep say to the winner of the election?
"We only have ayes for ewe."

What would you get if you crossed a tortoise and a sheep?

A turtle-neck sweater.

What would you get if you crossed a turtle and a boomerang?

Snappy comebacks.

What would you get if you crossed a skunk and a boomerang?

A terrible smell you can't get rid of.

Why did the skunk fail his swimming lesson?

He stank to the bottom of the pool.

What did the skunk say when the wind changed direction?

"It's coming back to me now."

Why did the boy stick a garden hose in the mound in his backyard?

He wanted to make a fountain out of a molehill.

What pet chicken once lived in the White House?

Teddy Roostervelt.

What did one hen say to another?

"Things aren't like they rooster be."

What did the hen say to the rooster?

Nothing. She just egged him on.

What did the Russian farmer name his hens?

The Brooders Karamazov.

What did Barbie, the play director, do when Chicken Little forgot his lines?

Barbie cued Chicken.

Why is an egg like a young horse?

It can't be used until it's broken.

What's the difference between a horse and a cloud?

One is reined up, and the other rains down.

Why did the horse stir his cereal with his hoof?

He wanted to feel his oats.

What happened to the itchy horse at post time?

He got scratched.

What did the horse say after eating all its hay?

"That's the last straw!"

What did the horse play in the movies?
Bit parts.

Why did the farmer put yeast in his horse's mane to keep birds from building nests in it?
Because yeast is yeast and nest is nest, and never the mane shall tweet.

What was the name of the pig farmer's company?
Oink, Inc.

Why are pig farmers hard to get along with?
They take everything for grunted.

What former pig farm is in the middle of New York City?
Central Pork.

What did one pig say to another on a hot day?
"I never sausage heat. In fact, I'm almost bacon."

Why do some sausages have meat at one end and corn-meal at the other?
Because it's hard to make both ends meat.

What pig tells long, dull stories?
A real boar (bore).

What is pigskin used for?
Holding pigs together.

Why was Miss Piggy's friend arrested?
Because he Kermitted a crime.

How do you know that the little snake caught a cold?
Because she adder viper nose.

What did one badger say to the other badger?
"Too badger sick."

Why did the man start a bee farm?
He liked keeping buzzy.

What does a bee wear to go jogging?
A swarm-up suit.

9. CRITTER LITTER

What is the purpose of the reindeer?
It makes the grass grow, sweetie.

What's the difference between a smelly dog and a dead stinging insect?
One is a seedy beast, and the other is a bee deceased.

What would you get if you crossed a bee and ground beef?
A humburger.

What would you get if you crossed a bee and a doorbell?
A humdinger.

What would you get if you crossed an elk and a mistake?
A cariboo-boo.

What is wholesale?
It's where a gopher goes to buy a new home.

What does "questionable" mean?
It's what the police do when they find a dead matador (question a bull).

What is black and white and red all over?
A blushing penguin.

How is a turtle like a cautious person?
He doesn't make any progress until he sticks his neck out.

What do you call a tortoise's excellent memory?
Turtle recall.

Why can't tortoises keep secrets?
They are turtle-tales (tattle-tales).

Why wouldn't the man buy any Christmas seals?
Because he didn't know how to feed them.

What did the beaver say to the tree?
"It's been nice gnawing you."

What did the man from Mars say to the cat?
"Take me to your litter."

What did one amoeba say to another?
"Don't bacilli."

Why did the sheep become a comedian?
Because he told baaaad jokes.

What happened to the sheep that fell in a vat of chocolate?
He became a Hershey baaaa.

Why did the baseball umpire retire?
Because his Seeing Eye dog died.

What happened when the bull gored Juan, the golfer?
The bull made a hole in Juan.

What would you get if you crossed a baseball player and a hunting dog?
A good retriever that chases flies and runs home when it sees the catcher.

What would you get if you crossed a yellow hunting dog and a short-wave radio?
A golden receiver.

What would you get if you crossed a lobster and a baseball player?

A pinch hitter.

What would you get if you crossed a vampire with a baseball player?

A bat boy.

Did you hear about the new cockroach doll?

You wind it up and it runs under the kitchen sink.

What goes "dot-dit-dit-dot-croak?"

A Morse toad.

What happened to the frog who parked in a wrong spot?

He got toad away.

What kind of shoes do frogs like?

Open-toad sandals.

What would you get if you crossed a woodchuck and Clint Eastwood?

A groundhog who's not afraid of his shadow.

What is a squirrel's favorite flower?

A forget-me-nut.

Why did the little rabbit's friend reject him after he shaved off his whiskers?

Because a bunny shaved (penny saved) is a bunny spurned (penny earned).

What did the bald rabbit wear?

A harepiece.

What did the butcher reply when a lady asked if she could buy just half a rabbit?

"No. I don't want to split hares."

What is a chicken's favorite breakfast?
Cereal that goes "snap, crackle and peep."

What would you get if you crossed a chicken and a banjo?
A self-plucking hen.

What soap do alligators use to control body odor?
A croco-Dial.

What did the girl cat reply when the boy cat said he loved her so much he would die for her?
"How many times?"

What happened to the dog who ate table scraps?
He got splinters in his tongue.

What was the pet grooming shop called?
The Laundra Mutt.

How do silent puppies feel?
Totally yelpless.

What did the shepherd shout when he saw a flock running wild?
"Abandon sheep!"

What would you get if you crossed a robin's leg, a haddock and a hand?
Birdsthigh (Bird's Eye) fish fingers.

What is a psychiatrist's favorite dinner?
Southern Freud chicken.

10. BUGGY BELLY LAUGHS

What did one insect say to the other insect?
"Stop bugging me!"

Who brought insects to the Old West?
Buffalo Bill Cootie.

What's the difference between a big embrace and a louse?
One is a bear hug, and the other is a hair bug.

What kind of insect is good at arithmetic?
An account-ant.

What do you call the body smell of an insect?
De-odor-ant.

How many insects does it take to make a landlord?
Ten-ants.

Have you heard about the new ant doll?
You wind it up and it goes on a picnic.

What did the ant and the bee do for fun?
They went on a buggy ride.

What is a bee's favorite song?
"Stinging in the rain."

What did the mother bee say to the baby bee?
"Beehive yourself!"

What did the bee say to her nosy neighbor?
"Mind your own bee's nest (business)."

Why did the worker bees go on strike?
They wanted more honey and shorter flowers.

What happened to the bee that visited too many flowers?
It suffered from high bud pressure.

What medicine do bees take when they're ill?
Anti-bee-otics.

Where do sick hornets go?
To the waspital.

How many insects are mentioned in the most famous
line from Shakespeare's *Hamlet*?
Four. "Two bees or not two bees . . ."

What's worse than a centipede with ingrown toenails?
A turtle with claustrophobia.

What do you get if you cross a centipede and a parrot?
A walkie-talkie.

What would you get if you crossed an octopus and a
centipede?
A pet that costs an arm and a leg.

What would you get if you crossed a pig and a centipede?

Bacon and legs.

What did the mother firefly say to her daughter?

"You're bright for your age."

What insect got an A in English?

A spelling bee.

What was the caterpillar's New Year's resolution?

It promised to turn over a new leaf.

What do you get if you cross an insect and a rabbit?

A bug's bunny.

What do librarians use bookworms for?

Bait.

What's greenish-brown and can jump a mile a minute?

A grasshopper with hiccups.

What would you get if you crossed a rabbit, a grasshopper and a cowboy?

Hopalong Grassidy.

What would you get if you crossed an absent-minded professor and an insect?

A forget-me-gnat.

What's the difference between a coyote and a flea?

One howls on the prairie and the other prowls on the hairy.

What would you get if you crossed a large elk and an insect?

A moose-quito.

What goes dit dit dot dit and bites?

A Morse-quito.

What does a religious mosquito do?

First it sings over you and then it preys on you.

What did one mosquito say to the other mosquito, after landing on Robinson Crusoe?

"I'm leaving now, but I'll see you on Friday."

What did the bug say to the rose?

"Hi, Bud!"

What did the rose reply?

"Bug off!"

11. ZOO'S WHO?

What book is about famous animals?

"Who's Zoo."

What do you call false teeth for zoo creatures?

Animal clackers.

Why did the zookeeper get in trouble for feeding the monkeys?

He fed them to the lions.

What would you get if you crossed a hyena and a chameleon?

Dr. Chuckle and Mr. Hide.

What would you get if you crossed a hyena and a vampire?

An animal that laughs at the sight of blood.

What would you get if you crossed a vampire and a vegetable?

Something that tries to get blood from a turnip.

What weighs four tons, eats peanuts, and lives in Southern California?

L. A. Phant.

What is big, gray, and goes choo-choo-choo?

An elephant with hay fever.

What is the last thing an elephant wants to hear from its dentist?

Tuscaloosa.

How did the elephant wash its tusks?

With Ivory Soap.

What's the best way to raise an elephant?

Use a crane.

What would you get if you crossed a shag carpet and an elephant?

A great big pile in your living room.

What do you get if you cross a contortionist and an elephant?

Someone who can tickle his own ivories.

Why are there so many elephant riddles?

Because it's never hard to find a new wrinkle.

What's the difference between elephant eggs and giraffe eggs?

Everyone likes elephant yolks.

What do zoo animals write on high walls?

Giraffiti (graffiti).

Why do giraffes have such small appetites?

Because a little goes a long way.

What would you get if you crossed a giraffe and an ostrich?

An animal that really sticks its neck out.

Can a giraffe get a sore throat from getting its feet wet?

Yes, but not until the following week.

What is worse than a giraffe with a sore throat?

One with a stiff neck.

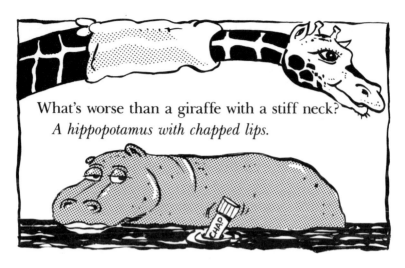

What's worse than a giraffe with a stiff neck?
A hippopotamus with chapped lips.

What weighs over a ton and puts people to sleep?
A hypno-potamus.

What weighs over a ton and thinks it's always sick?
A hippo-chondriac.

Who did the newspaper send to cover the zoo story?
A cub reporter.

What kind of fur coats did Adam and Eve wear?
Bearskins (bare skins).

If the alphabet goes from A to Z, then what goes from Z to A?
Zebra.

What do you get if you cross a zebra and a pig?
Striped sausages.

What's black and white and red all over?
An embarrassed zebra.

What's black and white and blue all over?
A zebra in an ice box.

What did the silly kid name her pet zebra?
Spot.

How would you describe a black cat walking over a zebra crossing?
Now you see it—now you don't.

What kind of ox can do many types of work?
A yak-of-all-trades.

Why are oxen such a pain to have around?
Because it's always yak, yak, yak.

What's the difference between a kangaroo and a lumberjack?
One hops and chews, and the other chops and hews.

What is a kangaroo's favorite breakfast?
Pouched eggs.

What is a kangaroo's favorite dinner?
Hop Suey.

How was the baby kangaroo kidnapped?
The mother had her pocket picked.

What would you get if you crossed two antelopes and some underwear?
Gnus' briefs.

What do you get if you cross cocoa and a big elk?
Chocolate moose.

12. JEST FOR THE HALIBUT

What language do fish speak?
Finnish.

What is a baby fish's favorite game?
Salmon Says.

What game do young fish like playing?
Carps and robbers.

Why do fish hate Coca-Cola?
Because it's the reel thing.

What kind of snack do fish eat?
Peanut butter and jellyfish sandwiches.

What's the difference between a fisherman and a lazy student?

One baits his hooks, and the other hates his books.

Why is a fisherman more honest than a shepherd?

A fisherman lives by hook, but a shepherd lives by crook.

Why don't fishermen use money?

Because they use credit cods.

What did one fisherman reply when the other said he got a haddock?

"Why don't you take an aspirin?"

What do you call the main doctor in a fish hospital?

The chief lobstertrician.

What was the crab's favorite musical show?
  "Fiddler on the Reef."

Why was the crab arrested?
  It was always pinching things.

Say this 5 times fast:
Selfish shellfish.

Why did the boy eat a lot of shellfish?
  For mussel tone.

Why did the octopus go to the doctor?
  Because he was a crazy mixed-up squid.

Why did the swordfish go to the doctor?
  He had a duel personality.

What did the baby whale say to its mother?
  "I don't feel whale."

What is stranger than seeing a shrimp roll?
  Seeing a clam bake.

Why did one shrimp crash into another shrimp?
  It was accident prawn.

Why was the electric eel arrested?
  It was brought up on charges.

What did the electric eel do at church?
  It shocked everyone.

MAN: How did you come to fall in the lake?
BOY: I didn't come to fall in. I came to fish.

Why are fish smarter than people?
  Have you ever seen a fish spend a lot of money to hook a man?

What do shoemakers have to do with fish?
  They use soles and eels.

What's the difference between a fisherman and a farmer?
  A fisherman puts the carp before the horse.

Why was a dolphin feeder hired at the zoo?
  To serve a porpoise.

What did the chef at the seafood restaurant say?
  "We fry harder."

What do the restroom signs say at a seafood restaurant?
  Buoys and Gulls.

What is a fish's favorite song?
  "Mackerel the Knife."

What is an alligator's favorite song?
  "Rock Around the Croc."

What is a mermaid?
A deep-she fish.

What's furry, meows, and chases mice under water?
A catfish.

What is the fiercest fish in the ocean?
Codzilla.

Who was the famous pirate octopus?
Captain Squid.

Where do homeless fish end up?
On squid roe.

What sign did the nuclear scientist hang on his office door?
"Gone Fission."

Why was the train station called Fish Hook?
Because it was at the end of the line.

What's the difference between a marine biologist and a dog?
One tags a whale, and the other wags a tail.

What do whales like to chew?
Blubber gum.

Who was the strongest man in the world?
Jonah—even the whale couldn't keep him down.

Why did the whale let Jonah go?
Because it couldn't stomach him.

What was the favorite seafood of King Arthur and his knights?
Swordfish.

How did short Pilgrims arrive in America?
In shrimp boats.

What wears white sheets and hates other fish?
The Ku Klux Clam.

What did the waiter reply when a customer asked for a nice lobster tail?

"Once upon a time there was a nice lobster . . ."

What did one herring say to the other herring?

"Am I my brother's kipper?"

What did the herring say to the whale?

"Am I my blubber's kipper?"

What do you get if you cross haddock and tiny computer parts?

Fish and chips.

What is a cannibal's favorite meal?

Fish and chaps.

What is a sea monster's favorite meal?

Fish and ships.

What's the difference between a newspaper and a radio?
You can't wrap fish and chips in a radio.

What would you get if you crossed a seafood restaurant
and antique furniture?
Fish and Chippendale.

What horror movie co-stars the Loch Ness monster and
a shark?
"Loch Jaws."

What is a shark's favorite hobby?
Anything he can sink his teeth into.

Why won't a shark attack a lawyer?
Because of professional courtesy.

What did the sharks do when the Weight Watchers went
swimming?
They chewed the fat.

How did the fish keep missing the fisherman's nets?
He was the sole survivor.

How did the fish go into business together?
They started on a small scale.

How do fish travel to work?
In carp pools.

What's worse than a rhinoceros on water skis?
A porcupine on a rubber raft.

What did Noah say to his two sons who were fishing from the ark?
"Take it easy on the bait, boys. I only have two worms."

13. FLYING HIGH

What did the parrot say to the frog?
"Polly wants a croaker."

Where do baby birds put their money?
In the stork market.

What costume does a dancing parrot wear?
A cocka-tutu.

Why didn't the parrot say a word for ten years?
It was stuffed.

What did the parrot say when he saw a duck?
"Polly wants a quacker."

What would you get if you crossed a parrot and a woodpecker?

A bird that talks in Morse code.

What would you get if you crossed a parrot and a homing pigeon?

A bird that asks its way home if it gets lost.

What would you get if you crossed a woodpecker and a homing pigeon?

A bird that knocks on your door before delivering the message.

What would you get if you crossed a pigeon and some Army generals?

A military coo.

What's the difference between a pigeon and a farmer?

The pigeon can still make a deposit on a new tractor.

What did one pigeon say to another while flying over a baseball game?

"I've put everything I have on the home team."

What bird has no wings?

A tomahawk.

What would happen if you crossed a mink and a bird?

You'd see the fur fly.

What do you get if you cross a bullet and a tree with no leaves?

A cartridge in a bare tree.

What did Santa Claus tell his reindeer?

"If you don't behave, I may get a gnu sleigh."

Why did the man buy an ice cream cone for the chirping birds?

So he could still two birds with one cone (kill two birds with one stone).

What did one bird say to another after seeing a jet fly by?

"I'd fly that fast too if my tail were on fire."

Why did the robin get in trouble?
He did it all for a lark.

What did the pelican say after a huge fish dinner?

"Well, that certainly fills the bill."

What's the difference between a butcher and a night owl?

One weighs a steak, the other stays awake.

How did the girl gain so much weight eating like a bird?

She ate a peck at a time.

What do you get if you cross an oyster and an owl?

Pearls of wisdom.

What did the hen do when it saw a large order of Kentucky Fried Chicken?

It kicked the bucket.

What is a chicken's favorite dessert?

Layer cake.

What did the sign on the chicken farm say?

"Roost in peace."

What happened when the duck flew upside down?

It had a quack up.

Why do ducks have to fight depression?

Because they often get down in the mouth.

Where do geese invest their money?

In savings and loons.

What would you get if you crossed a pastry and bird meat?

An eclair du loon (clair de lune).

What breakfast would you get if you crossed the Panama Canal and an ocean bird?

Locks and bay gulls (lox and bagels).

What happened to the woman who had ten children?

She went stork raving mad.

What did the artist call his painting of a canary?

Mother's Whistler.

What have you got when two canaries pay for their own meals?

Dutch tweet.

What do you call a canary that flies into a dessert?
Tweetie Pie.

What do you call a canary that joins the Ice Capades?
A cheep skate.

What kind of canary does a bargain hunter shop for?
A cheaper cheeper.

Why do some fisherman use helicopters to catch their bait?
Because the whirly bird gets the worm.

Why are cheerful birds healthier than gloomy ones?
Because the surly bird catches the germ.

What is a pheasant under glass in a restaurant?
A small bird with a large bill.

What did the pet store owner say when the boy asked if he could buy a bird and have the bill sent?
"No, you'll have to take the whole bird."

What is the favorite hymn of fish?
"Nearer, my cod, to thee."

What did one tonsil say to another?
"Winter must be over. Here comes a swallow."

14. TOUGHER & TOUGHER

What did the toad say to the vet?
  "What's the frognosis (prognosis)?"

Where do whales learn how to spell?
  In a Moby Dicktionary.

Why did the minister give some of his chickens away?
  Because his coop (cup) runneth over.

What did the farmer do when his chickens flew away?
  He tried to recoop (recoup) his losses.

Why did the boy complain about having chicken dinners so often?
  He got tired of biting the pullet (bullet).

What kind of eggs do cattle rustlers like?
Poached.

What cowardly Washington congressman sells tunafish?
Chicken of D.C.

What lizard tells jokes and changes colors?
A stand-up chameleon.

Why is hot bread like a caterpillar?
Because it is the grub that makes the butter fly.

What's the difference between a father gorilla, a bald-headed man, an orphan and a crown prince?
One is a hairy parent, one has no hair apparent, one has ne'er a parent, and one is an heir apparent.

What happened when the king allowed wild animals to run loose?
The reign was called on account of game.

What happened to the long-necked bird that was a social outcast?
It was ostrichized.

What happened when some animals in the ark multiplied?
Noah became the first man to have bred his cast upon the waters.

Why were some of the animals in the ark angry?
Because the Captain acted like a Noah-it-all.

What animal was first out of the ark?
I don't know. But Noah came fourth (forth).

Why was Noah the world's first financial investor?
He floated his stock, while everyone else was being liquidated.

What would you call a story about a dog that runs after a stick for three miles?
Too far-fetched.

What happened to the boy who made mountains out of molehills?
Whenever he made a mistake, it was a butte (beaut).

How can you use "conscience stricken" in a sentence?
"Don't conscience strickens before they hatch."

What do you get if you cross an insomniac, an agnostic and a dyslexic?
Someone who stays awake all night wondering about the meaning of dog.

Who rode a horse up a hill to fetch a pail of water?
Jockey and Jill.

What's the difference between fast teaching and a groomed pony?
One is a hurried course, and the other is a curried horse.

When does a horse eat best?
When it doesn't have a bit in its mouth.

Why is a tongue like a horse?
It runs fastest when it carries the least weight.

Why did the farmer bottle feed his horses after birth?
Because a foal and his mummy are soon parted.

Who was Eric the Red?
A Norse of a different color.

What's the difference between a lama, a llama and a three-L lllama?
The first is a monk, the second is an animal, and the third is a huge fire.

What happened when the French girl threw three cats in the lake?
Un, deux, trois cats sank (quatre cinq).

What Government department finds lost cats?
The Bureau of Missing Purrsians.

What do crazy cats like to drink?

Catatonic.

What happened when a woodchuck escaped from a pet shop in a shopping center?

The store owner said, "The chuck is in the mall."

What do you get when a goat eats a rabbit?

A hare in the butter.

What do you call an ugly rabbit that sits on your forehead?

Unsightly facial hare.

What happened to the bee that flew in a cow's ear and ended up in a pail of milk?

It went in one ear and out the udder.

How many babies did the mother cow have?

About heifer dozen.

What's the difference between a dark cow and a war for the throne?

One is brown cattle, and the other is a crown battle.

Why doesn't Sweden export cattle?

Because it wants to keep its Stockholm.

What happened after the actor spent a year in stock?

The cattle finally objected.

What do you call cows that are launched into space in a rocket?

The herd shot 'round the world.

What did one zookeeper say to the other zookeeper?

"Show me a home where the buffalo roam, and I'll show you a messy house."

What did the ostrich say after arriving late to a party where everyone had their heads buried in the sand?

"Where is everybody?"

INDEX

Aardvarks, 5, 22
Abalone, 12
Actor, 93
Adam and Eve, 70
Adder, 40, 55
Agnostic, 90
Alligator, 11, 35, 61, 76
Alphabet, 70
Alps, 44
Amoeba, 9, 58
Animal: kingdom, 5;
    strongest, 34; stuffed,
    31
Anteaters, 5
Antelope, 37, 72
Ants, 5, 8, 17, 22, 62, 63
Apes, 8, 41
Appetites, 69
Ark, 89, 90
Arthur, King, 78
Artist, 86
Asp, 36
Astronaut, 38
Athletes, 50
Athlete's foot, 8
Axe, 10

Babies, 92
Bacon, 55, 65
Badger, 55
Bag, 66
Banjo, 61
Bargain hunter, 87
Baseball, 58, 59; game, 83
Bats, 10
Bears, 6, 7, 13, 14, 31,
    37, 46
Beaver, 57
Bees, 6, 7, 14, 49, 55, 56,
    63, 64, 65, 92
Beef, 56
Bell, 41
Bic, 46
Bill, 87
Birds, 8, 16, 19, 35, 54,
    82, 83, 84, 85, 86, 87;
    and the bees, 51
Bison, 20
Blender, 16
Blood, 67, 68
Bloodhounds, 14
Blotter, 48
Boa constrictor, 36, 37
Boars, 16
Bobcat, 26
Body odor, 61
Books, 19, 67, 74
Boomerang, 52
Bo Peep, 29

Bowling, 25
Boxing, 16
Boy Scouts, 10
Bread, 89
Breakfast, 61, 72, 86
Breath, 9, 11
Breeding, 26
Broom, 41
Bucks, 33, 34, 38
Buffalo, 8, 20, 93; Bill, 62
Bugs, 38, 64, 65
Bull, 26, 57, 58
Bullet, 83
Burglar, cat, 26
Business, 81
Butcher, 60, 84

Cactus, 7
Cake, 85
Camels, 21
Camera, 11
Camping, 40
Canary, 7, 16, 86, 87
Candy, 13
Cannibal, 16, 32, 79
Cantaloupe, 32
Cards, playing, 19, 27
Carpenters, 39
Carpet, 69
Carrots, 11
Cars, 22, 42
Caterpillars, 6, 65, 89
Catfish, 77
Cats, 7, 23–28, 31, 34,
    57, 61, 71, 91, 92
Catskill Mountains, 28
Cattle, 32, 50, 51, 93;
    rustlers, 89
Cells, 9
Centipede, 8, 64, 65
Cereal, 61
Chameleon, 67
Checks, 39
Chef, 48, 76
Cheese, 48
Chickens, 10, 18, 19, 35,
    47, 53, 61, 85, 88, 89,
    90
Children, 86
Chili pepper, 33
Chippendale, 80
Chocolate, 58
Clam, 78; bake, 75
Claustrophobia, 27, 64
Clock, 19, 40; alarm, 7
Cloud, 53
Cockroach doll, 59
Cocoa, 72
Cod, 14, 19, 87

Cold, 55
Comedian, 13, 58
Comma, 23
Computer, 45, 79
Conscience, 90
Contortionist, 69
Corn, 7, 49
Costume, 82
Cowboy, 65
Cows, 20, 21, 32, 49, 50,
    92, 93
Coyote, 65
Crab, 75
Crocodile, 11, 12, 38
Crockpot, 48
Crow, 38
Crowd, 50
Crusoe, Robinson, 66

Dalmation, 8
Dancers, 41
Dates, 37; blind, 10
Deer, 33, 37, 39
Dentist, 30, 68
Deodorant, 62
Depression, 85
Dessert, 85, 87
Detectives, 27, 31
Diaper rash, 41
Dinners, 61, 84, 88
Dinosaurs, 14, 39
Doctor, 14, 41, 74, 75
Dogs, 8, 10, 14, 15, 17,
    19, 30–33, 48, 56, 58,
    61, 79, 90
Doll, 59, 63
Dolphins, 76
Donkey, 20, 35
Doorbell, 56
Dracula, 9, 19
Dragon, 12
Ducks, 5, 39, 46, 82, 85
Dwarfs, 11
Dyslexic, 90

Eastwood, Clint, 60
Eel, electric, 76
Eggs, 10, 39, 53, 69, 72,
    89
Egg whites, 41
Elephants, 8, 15, 44, 45,
    68, 69
Elk, 57, 66, 72
Embrace, 62
Exterminator, 31
Eyeglasses, 17

Factory, sardine, 35
Family tree, 37

Farm, chicken, 85
Farmer, 20, 49, 51, 53, 76, 83, 91
Fireflies, 49, 65
Fish, 19, 34, 61, 73, 76–82
Fisherman, 35, 74, 81, 87
Fishing, 76, 77, 81
Flamingos, 38
Fleas, 17, 43, 65
Flies, 18, 31, 58
Flowers, 60, 63
Football, 6, 21
Fox, 42
Frankenstein, 19
Frogs, 8, 17, 18, 46, 59
Fur coats, 70
Furniture, antique, 80

Games, 19, 20, 73, 89
Garbage, 46
Geese, 85
Generals, 83
Germs, 87
Ghosts, 10, 14
Giraffes, 69, 70
Gnat, 65
Gnus, 5, 22, 34, 37, 84
Goat, 16, 46, 92
Goat's milk, 30
Goldilocks, 37
Golfer, 58
Gopher, 57
Gorilla, 41, 45, 89
Grasshopper, 65
Great Dane, 15
Groundhog, 16, 60
Guest, bored, 17
Gulls, 86
Gum, 79

Haddock, 61, 74, 79
Haircut, 47
Hamlet, 64
Hares, splitting, 60
Hay, 53; bale of, 41
Helicopters, 87
Hen, 61, 85; *also see* Chicken
Herring, 78
Hiccups, 65
Hippopotamus, 70
Hobby, 80
Hopalong Cassidy, 65
Hornets, 64
Horse, 10, 16, 34, 39, 43, 53, 54, 90, 91; trainer, 42
Horseback riding school, 39
Hose, garden, 53

Hot dogs, 48
Hotel, 33; rooms, 13
Hunter, 37
Hyena, 67
Hymn, 87

Ice Capades, 87
Ice cream, 48; cone, 84
Iguana, 13
Infant, 32
Insect, 62, 66
Insomniac, 90

Jekyll, Dr., 19
Jet, 84
Jewelry, 26
Jokes, 58, 69, 89
Jonah, 79
Jungle, 31; gym, 22

Kangaroo, 30, 32, 71, 72
Kentucky Fried Chicken, 85
Kermit, 55
Killer, serial, 34
Kipper, 78
Kittens, 23
Knights, 12
Koala bears, 6

Lambs, 15, 29, 47
Landlord, 63
Language, 8, 73
Lark, 84
Lawnmower, 28
Lawyer, 80
Leopard, 25
Letters, 7
Lettuce, 42
Librarians, 65
Light bulb, 11
Lions, 25, 26, 67
Litterbug, 46
Lizards, 13, 89
Llama, 37, 91
Lobster, 59, 78
Loch Ness monster, 80
Locksmith, 19
Loons, 85, 86
Louse, 62
Lumberjack, 71
Lynx, 26

Magazine, 43, 50, 51
Mane, horse's, 54
Marine biologist, 79
Marine Corps, 41
Martian, 57
Matadors, 7, 57
Match, 27

Meal, 79, 86
Mechanic, car, 35
Medicine, 64
Memory, 57
Mermaid, 77
Mice, 5
Microwave, 9
Milk, 50
Mind-reading, 24
Minister, 14, 35, 88
Mink, 28, 83
Mistake, 57
Molehill, 53, 90
Monastery, 25
Money, 74, 82, 85
Monkey, 41, 45, 46, 67
Monster, 37; sea, 79
Moose, 5, 72
Morse code, 66
Moses, 43
Mosquito, 65, 66
Motorcyclist, 38
Motorist, 17
Mountains, 44, 90
Mouse, 44
Movies, 46, 54, 80
Musical, 45, 75
Musician, 41

Needle, 25
Newspaper, 20, 47, 70, 80; advice column, 27
New Year's resolution, 65
Nickel, 8
Noah, 7, 34, 43, 81, 89, 90
Novocaine, 30
Nuts, 6

Oats, 53
Ocean, 14, 20, 77; bird, 86
Octopus, 21, 40, 41, 64, 75, 77
Old West, 23, 62
Opera, 13
Orphan, 89
Ostrich, 30, 69, 89, 93
Otters, 33
Owl, night, 84
Ox, 71
Oyster, 84

Painter, 19
Panama Canal, 86
Pandas, 37
Parrots, 31, 45, 64, 82, 83
Pasta, 36
Pastimes, 7
Pastry, 86
Peacocks, 44

Pearls, 84
Peck, Gregory, 47
Pelican, 84
Penguin, 46, 57
Pens, 7
Pet grooming shop, 61
Pet shop, 92; owner, 87
Pheasant, 87
Photograph, 11
Pig, 16, 21, 46, 55, 65, 70; farmer, 54
Pigeon, 83
Piggy, Miss, 55
Pilgrims, 78
Pizza, 5
Policeman, 40
Poltergeist, 10
Pony, 90
Porcupines, 7, 33, 44, 81
Porpoise, 76
Potato crop, 49
Prince, crown, 89
Professor, absent-minded, 65
Psychiatrist, 24, 61
Publications, 19
Pullet, 88
Punctuality, 7
Puppies, 61

Rabbits, 11, 30, 31, 37, 42, 60, 65, 92
Races, 34, 38, 46, 53
Racing forms, 18
Radio, 80; short-wave, 58
Raft, 81
Rain, 26
Rats, 28
Readers, 26
Reign, 89
Reindeer, 12, 56, 84
Reptiles, 38
Rhinos, 22, 81
Robin, 61, 84
Roe, 77
Rogers, Buck, 38
Rooster, 48
Rose, 66

Saloon, 23
Sandwich, 46
Santa Claus, 84
Sardines, 35
Sausages, 55, 70
Scientist, nuclear, 77
Seafood, 78; restaurant, 76, 80

Seahorse, 49
Seals, 57
Secrets, 11, 29
Shark, 80, 81
Sheep, 10, 16, 20, 29, 37, 51, 52, 58, 61
Sheik, 50
Shellfish, 75
Shepherd, 61, 74
Shoemakers, 76
Shoes, 59
Shopping, 15, 87
Shrimp, 75
Singers, 13
Situation comedy, 16
Skate, 87
Skunks, 11, 14, 41, 52
Smell, 52
Smoking, 30
Snacks, 5, 73
Snakes, 13, 22, 36, 40, 55
Soap, 61
Soldiers, 21
Song, 37, 76
Spaghetti, 36
Spanking, 33
Spelling, 88; bee, 65
Squid, 75, 77
Squirrel, 33, 48, 60
Stamp, 20
Steak, 84
Steamroller, 24
Steroids, 50
Stiff neck, 69
Stockbroker, 35
Stork, 86
Strongest: animal, 34; man, 79
Student, lazy, 74
Stuffed animals, 31
Subway, 35
Surfing, 9
Swallow, 87
Sweater, 52
Sweden, 93
Swimming, 80; lesson, 52
Swordfish, 75, 78

Table: scraps, 61; tennis, 41
Tail, 27, 79, 84
Tailor, 42
Talking, 8
Tarzan, 22
Team, losing, 22
Teeth: false, 41, 67; picking your, 7
Telephone, 26, 38

Temper, 11
Termites, 12, 13
Tigers, 25
Toad, 59, 88; also see Frog
Tomahawk, 83
Tonsil, 87
Tortoise, 52, 57
Toy store, 31
Track star, 27
Tractor, 49
Train station, 79
Trampoline, 13
Travel, 42
Trees, 10, 57, 83
Tunafish, 89
Turkey, 18, 24, 30
Turtle, 52, 57, 64

Umpire, 58
Underwater, 72
Unicorn, 42
United Nations, 15

Vacation, 47, 66
Vampires, 9, 19, 33, 41, 59, 67, 68
VCR, 22
Vegetable, 68
Veterinarian, 30, 88
Viper, 55

Waiter, 78
War, 93; time, 37
Washing machine, 28
Water: polo, 16; skis, 81
Weevils, 14
Weight, 84; Watchers, 80
Werewolf, 14
Whales, 29, 75, 78, 79, 88
White House, 53
Wind, 52
Wine, 22
Wisdom, 84
Woodchuck, 60, 92
Woodpecker, 83
Worms, 81, 87
Writers, 26

Yak, 71
Yeast, 54

Zebra, 70, 71
Zoo, 46, 67, 70, 76; keeper, 37, 45, 67, 93